TEETH

Thanks to the American Dental Association for its help in verifying facts for this book

First Steck-Vaughn Edition 1992

Copyright © 1989 American Teacher Publications

Published by Steck-Vaughn Company

Library of Congress number: 89-3844

Library of Congress Cataloging in Publication Data.

Maloy, Jacqueline.
  Teeth/Jacqueline Maloy; illustrated by Susan Miller.

  (Real readers)
  Summary: A science book for beginning readers describing the basic structure of teeth, how they grow, why they fall out, and how to take care of them.
  1. Teeth—Juvenile literature. [1. Teeth.] I. Miller, Susan, ill. II. Title. III. Series.
QP88.6.M35 1989   612'.311—dc19   89-3844

ISBN 0-8172-3520-5   hardcover library binding

ISBN 0-8114-6722-8   softcover binding

      6 7 8 9 0   01 00 99 98

TEETH

by Jacqueline Maloy
illustrated by Susan Miller

STECK-VAUGHN
C O M P A N Y
A Subsidiary of National Education Corporation

What do you see when you give a big grin?

You see your teeth!

A tooth has a crown and it has roots.

The crown is what you see when you look in your mouth. You use the crown of your tooth to eat your food.

You can't see the roots of a tooth when you look in your mouth. They are inside your gums. But the roots have a job, too. They keep your tooth in place. The roots keep your teeth from falling out.

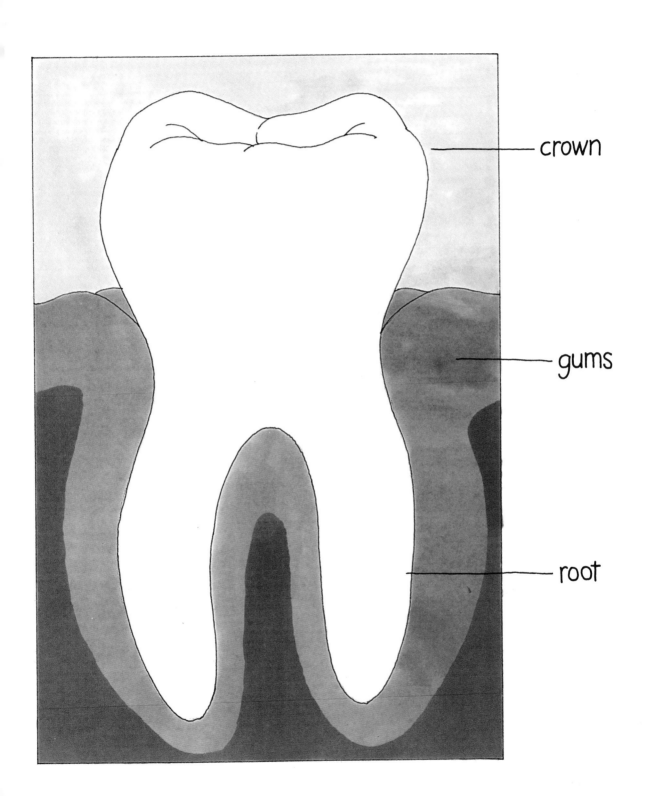

crown

gums

root

Do you see teeth when a new baby gives a big grin? No! Do you see teeth when you look in a new baby's mouth? No!

Does this mean that a new baby doesn't have teeth?

A new baby does not have teeth like yours. A new baby has tooth buds. Tooth buds are very little teeth. They are inside the baby's gums. That is why you cannot see them when you look in the baby's mouth.

When a baby is about 6 months old, he or she will get a first tooth. As the baby grows, the tooth buds grow, too. One by one, they grow so big that they cut through the baby's gums.

By the time the baby is about 2 years old, the baby will have 20 teeth. This set of teeth is called the baby teeth.

Baby Teeth

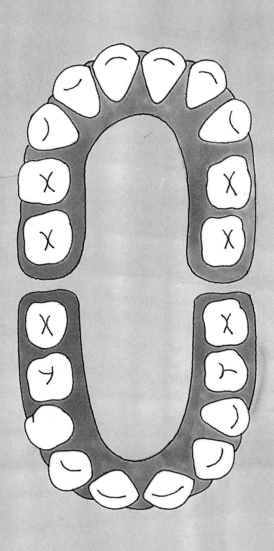

When you get to be about 6 years old, something starts to happen to your baby teeth. They start to fall out!

One by one, your baby teeth will fall out. Then one by one, new teeth will cut through your gums. The new teeth make up a set of teeth called the permanent teeth.

By the time you are about 12, you will have lost all of your baby teeth, and you will have at least 20 new permanent teeth.

By the time you are 21, you will have all of your permanent teeth. You will have 32 permanent teeth when they all come in.

Permanent Teeth

The permanent teeth start out as buds inside your gums, just the way your baby teeth did. But why do your baby teeth fall out? And why do your permanent teeth come in?

When you were 3 years old, the roots of your baby teeth started to get smaller and smaller. It takes a very long time, but when a baby tooth has no roots left, it falls out.

The baby tooth leaves a place in your mouth for a tooth bud to grow into a tooth. A permanent tooth will grow in to take the baby tooth's place.

As you grow, your mouth gets bigger. So you need bigger teeth. Your permanent teeth are bigger than your baby teeth. They have to last for more time, too.

If a permanent tooth falls out, a new tooth will not grow in its place. So you need to take good care of your teeth.

One thing that helps your teeth is eating good foods. Some foods like milk and apples are good for your teeth.

Foods that have lots of sugar in them, like cakes and jams, are bad for your teeth. The sugar clings to your teeth. This can lead to little holes in your teeth. These holes are called cavities. The cavities will get bigger and bigger if they are not fixed.

Foods That Are Good for Teeth

| apples | milk | carrots | nuts |

Foods That Are Bad for Teeth

| cake | jam | soda | candy |

Brushing is good for your teeth, too.
Brushing with a toothbrush after each
meal keeps your teeth clean. It keeps
food off your teeth so that you will not get
cavities.

Flossing helps clean teeth, too. You can
floss after you brush.

A dentist can help you take care of your teeth. At the dentist's, your teeth will be cleaned. The dentist will look at your teeth to see if there are cavities. If there are cavities, the dentist will fix them.

Your dentist will tell you how to take good care of your teeth. Your dentist may give you a new toothbrush to help you keep your teeth clean!

Now you know some things about teeth. You know where teeth come from. You know how teeth grow. And you know how to take care of your teeth.

You have a lot to grin about!

So give a big grin!

Sharing the Joy of Reading

Beginning readers enjoy reading books on their own. Reading a book is a worthwhile activity in and of itself for a young reader. However, a child's reading can be even more rewarding if it is shared. This sharing can enhance your child's appreciation — both of the book and of his or her own abilities.

Now that your child has read **Teeth,** you can help extend your child's reading experience by encouraging him or her to:

- Retell the story or key concepts presented in this story in his or her own words. The retelling can be oral or written.

- Create a picture of a favorite character, event, or concept from this book.

- Express his or her own ideas and feelings about the subject of this book and other things he or she might want to know about this subject.

Here is a special activity that you and your child can do together to further extend the appreciation of this book: You and your child can make a toothbrush holder. Start by talking about how you can decorate a toothbrush holder, such as with drawings or magazine pictures of tooth-care procedures, abstract or realistic illustrations, stickers, or other designs. Then supply an empty, clean, six-ounce frozen juice can with one end still in place, and a piece of construction paper cut to size for wrapping around the can. Ask your child to decorate the paper as planned and then glue it to the can. Help your child preserve the artwork by covering the can with clear contact paper or plastic wrap. The toothbrush holder is now ready to use.